SUPER SCIENCE FEATS

THE FIRST FLIGHT

by Nikole Brooks Bethea

pogo

Ideas for Parents and Teachers

Pogo Books let children practice reading informational text while introducing them to nonfiction features such as headings, labels, sidebars, maps, and diagrams, as well as a table of contents, glossary, and index.

Carefully leveled text with a strong photo match offers early fluent readers the support they need to succeed.

Before Reading

- "Walk" through the book and point out the various nonfiction features. Ask the student what purpose each feature serves.
- Look at the glossary together. Read and discuss the words.

Read the Book

- Have the child read the book independently.
- Invite him or her to list questions that arise from reading.

After Reading

- Discuss the child's questions. Talk about how he or she might find answers to those questions.
- Prompt the child to think more. Ask: What did you know about the Wright brothers and the first flight before you read this book? What else would you like to learn?

Pogo Books are published by Jump!
5357 Penn Avenue South
Minneapolis, MN 55419
www.jumplibrary.com

Copyright © 2019 Jump!
International copyright reserved in all countries. No part of this book may be reproduced in any form without written permission from the publisher.

Library of Congress Cataloging-in-Publication Data

Names: Bethea, Nikole Brooks, author.
Title: The first flight / by Nikole Brooks Bethea.
Description: Minneapolis, MN: Jump!, Inc., [2018].
Series: Super science feats | "Pogo Books are published by Jump!" | Audience: Ages 7-10.
Includes bibliographical references and index.
Identifiers: LCCN 2017050063 (print)
LCCN 2017049130 (ebook)
ISBN 9781624968693 (ebook)
ISBN 9781624968686 (hardcover: alk. paper)
Subjects: LCSH: Wright, Orville, 1871-1948–Juvenile literature. | Wright, Wilbur, 1867-1912–Juvenile literature. | Wright Flyer (Airplane) – Juvenile literature. | Aeronautics–History–Juvenile literature.
Classification: LCC TL540.W7 (print) | LCC TL540.W7 B48 2018 (ebook) | DDC 629.13009–dc23
LC record available at https://lccn.loc.gov/2017050063

Editor: Kristine Spanier
Book Designer: Michelle Sonnek

Photo Credits: Library of Congress/Superstock, cover, 8-9; THPStock/Shutterstock, cover (clouds); Robert T. McCall/NASA, 1; Lefteris Papaulakis/Shutterstock, 3; Chronicle/Alamy, 4; Pictorial Press Ltd/Alamy, 5; Hi-Story/Alamy, 6-7; Everett Historical/Shutterstock, 10-11; Dorling Kindersley/Exactostock-4268/Superstock, 12; Library of Congress/Superstock, 13; Chronicle/Alamy, 14-15; phive/Shutterstock, 16; Kamenetskiy Konstantin/Shutterstock, 17; IM_photo/Shutterstock, 18-19; Lulub/Shutterstock, 20-21; Lane Oatey/Blue Jean Images/Getty, 23.

Printed in the United States of America at Corporate Graphics in North Mankato, Minnesota.

TABLE OF CONTENTS

CHAPTER 1
Powered Flight 4

CHAPTER 2
Experimenting with Flight 12

CHAPTER 3
The Science of Flight 16

ACTIVITIES & TOOLS
Try This! 22
Glossary 23
Index 24
To Learn More 24

CHAPTER 1

POWERED FLIGHT

The flying machine sat at the top of the hill. It was unhooked. It rolled down the track. The **engine** started. The plane shot off the rail. It was in the air!

Orville

Wilbur

The plane was flying! It was December 17, 1903, at 10:35 a.m. Orville and Wilbur Wright, two brothers, had flown the first successful airplane. It was in Kitty Hawk, North Carolina.

CHAPTER 1

That first flight lasted just 12 seconds. Orville flew the plane 120 feet (37 meters). The brothers made four flights that day. Which one was the best? Wilbur flew it 852 feet (260 m). It flew for 59 seconds.

CHAPTER 1

The brothers called the machine the Flyer. The pilot laid on the **frame**. The controls connected to a **cradle**. He leaned side to side. Why? So he could move the wings and the **rudder**. The lever in his left hand moved the plane up and down.

DID YOU KNOW?

The Flyer's frame was made of wood. Cotton cloth covered it. The wingspan was 40 feet (12 m). That is the length of a school bus!

The 1903 Flyer was powered. It had two **propellers**. Each was eight feet (2.4 m) in **diameter**. A gasoline engine turned the propellers. They rotated in opposite directions.

DID YOU KNOW?

The brothers continued to develop a better airplane. In 1905, Wilbur circled a field 30 times. He flew 39 minutes. The flight totaled 24.5 miles (39 kilometers).

CHAPTER 1

CHAPTER 2
EXPERIMENTING WITH FLIGHT

The brothers' first flights were not with planes. They designed their control system using a box kite.

Then they built a small **glider**. They took it to Kitty Hawk. They launched the glider. The control system worked! But the glider could not carry a man.

CHAPTER 2

Next, the brothers tested a larger glider. They piloted glides up to 400 feet (122 m). The controls performed worse than before.

They flew their third glider in 1902. It had a new, movable rudder on it. Finally, the brothers could control it. They made glides up to 622 feet (190 m). The flights lasted up to 26 seconds.

The Wright brothers **patented** their design.

rudder

CHAPTER 2 — 15

CHAPTER 3
THE SCIENCE OF FLIGHT

Flight is a balancing act. **Forces** push and pull on the plane. How does it stay in the air?

Thrust is a forward force. It pushes the plane. The engine provides thrust. The opposite force is **drag**. It resists the plane moving through air. To move forward, thrust must be greater than drag.

CHAPTER 3

Mass is the amount of matter in the plane. **Weight** is the measure of **gravity** pulling down on the plane's mass.

Wings create **lift** as the plane flies through air. Lift is an upward force. To fly, lift must be greater than the force of gravity.

TAKE A LOOK!

Thrust was created by propellers in the 1903 Wright Flyer. A gas engine turned the propellers.

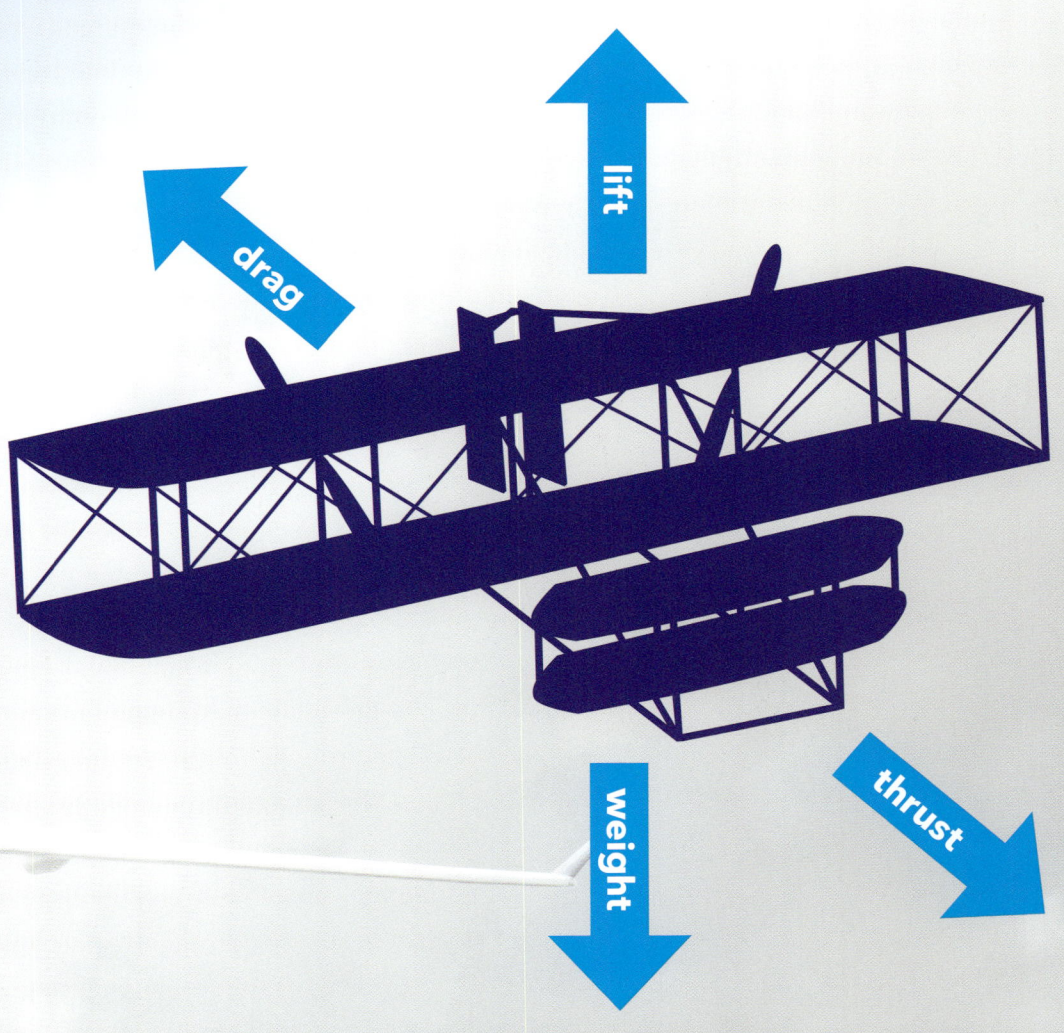

It has been more than 100 years since the first flight. Today, we depend on flight for many things. Like the Wright brothers, we continue to improve the airplane.

DID YOU KNOW?

When was the longest nonstop flight? February 2006. Steve Fossett flew almost 77 hours. How far did he go? More than 26,000 miles (42,000 km)!

CHAPTER 3

ACTIVITIES & TOOLS

TRY THIS!

EXPERIMENT WITH FLIGHT

Change the design of a paper airplane to see how its flight is affected.

Figure 1

Figure 2

What You Need:
- two pieces of paper
- pencil
- ruler
- tape measure
- scissors

1. Fold one sheet of paper into a standard airplane as in Figure 1.
2. Go to a long hallway or large open area. Lay the ruler on the ground as a starting line.
3. Put your toe on the starting line and throw the airplane.
4. Measure the distance from the starting line to the tip of the airplane. Record it on the other sheet of paper.
5. Repeat two more times holding the plane in the same spot each time and throwing with the same force. Did it fly approximately the same distance each time?
6. Now change the design to add drag. Find the middle ridge on the plane where the wings meet. Cut slits from the back of the plane one inch (2.5 centimeters) long where each wing meets the ridge. Fold these sections up as in Figure 2.
7. Repeat steps 3 through 5 again. How do the different designs change the flight of the airplane?

GLOSSARY

cradle: The movable support that held the pilot and adjusted the direction of the wings and rudder on the Flyer.

diameter: The length of a straight line through the center of a circle, connecting opposite sides.

drag: The force acting on an airplane to slow it down as it moves through the air.

engine: A machine that changes energy into movement.

forces: Actions that produce, stop, or change the movement of an object.

frame: A basic structure that provides the support for an airplane.

glider: A light aircraft without an engine.

gravity: The force that pulls things toward the center of Earth and keeps them from floating away.

lift: An upward force that overcomes the weight of an aircraft to keep it in the sky.

mass: The amount of matter in an object.

patented: To have obtained a legal document that gives the inventor of an item the sole rights to manufacture or sell it.

propellers: Sets of rotating blades that provide force to move a plane through air.

rudder: A flat piece attached to the rear of an aircraft for steering.

thrust: The force, created by engines, that drives an aircraft forward.

weight: The amount of force on an object due to gravity.

INDEX

box kite 12
cradle 8
drag 17, 19
engine 4, 11, 17, 19
Flyer 8, 11, 19
Fossett, Steve 21
frame 8
glider 13, 14
gravity 18
Kitty Hawk 5, 13
lift 18, 19
mass 18
patented 14
propellers 11, 19
rudder 8, 14
thrust 17, 19
track 4
weight 18, 19
wingspan 8
Wright brothers 5, 7, 8, 11, 12, 14, 21

TO LEARN MORE

Learning more is as easy as 1, 2, 3.
1) Go to www.factsurfer.com
2) Enter "firstflight" into the search box.
3) Click the "Surf" button to see a list of websites.

With factsurfer, finding more information is just a click away.